SCIENCE ENCOUNTERS

Movies

CHRIS OXLADE

© 1997 Rigby Education
Published by Rigby Interactive Library, an imprint of Rigby Education,
division of Reed Elsevier, Inc.
500 Coventry Lane
Crystal Lake, IL 60014

All rights reserved. No part of this publication may be reproduced,
stored in a retrieval system, or transmitted in any form or by any means,
electronic or mechanical, including photocopying, recording, taping,
or any information storage and retrieval system without permission
in writing from the publisher.

Interiors designed by **AMR**
Illustrations by Art Construction
Printed in the United Kingdom

00 99 98 97 96
10 9 8 7 6 5 4 3 2 1

Library of Congress Cataloging- in Publication Data
Oxlade, Chris.
   Movies / Chris Oxlade.
      p.   cm. – (Science encounters)
Includes bibliographical references and index.
Summary: Explains some of the scientific principles behind the various
techniques and processes involved in making movies.
      ISBN 1-57572-088-4
   1. Cinematography–Juvenile literature. 2. Motion pictures–
Production and direction–Juvenile literature.
[1. Cinematography. 2. Motion pictures–Production and direction.]
I. Title. II. Series.
TR851.094 1997
778.5'3–dc20   96-27563
                                                                       CIP
                                                                       AC

Acknowledgments
The publisher would like to thank the following for permission to reproduce photographs.
The Ronald Grant Archive, p. 4 (bottom), p. 12 (bottom), p. 24, p. 26; BFI Stills, Posters and
Designs, p. 5, p. 10, p. 17, p. 18, p. 20, p .22; Michael Holford, p. 6, p. 7 (top); The Science
Museum/Science and Society Picture Library, p. 7 (bottom); Nick Yates, p. 8, p. 14, p. 21;
The Kobal Collection, p. 12 (top), p .16, p. 28, p. 29; National Museum of Photography, Film
and Television, p. 25; JNTO, p. 27

Every effort has been made to contact copyright holders of any material reproduced in this book.
Any omissions will be rectified in subsequent printings if notice is given to the publisher.

CONTENTS

Science in Movies 4

Moving Pictures 6

On Film 8

Soundtracks 10

Bright Lights 12

The Road From Camera to Theater 14

Special Effects 16

Stunt Action 18

Animated Movies 20

On Screen 22

Big Pictures 24

More Movie Tricks 26

Movies About Science 28

Glossary 30

Fact File 31

Index 32

SCIENCE IN MOVIES

As you sit in your comfortable theater seat, eating popcorn and watching the latest blockbuster movie, you probably don't think about how the movie was actually made. In this book, you can find out how science is used on a movie **set,** when the movie is edited, and when it is shown in the theater. You can also find out how science and technology make amazing special effects possible.

Pictures and Sound

The word *movie* is short for *moving picture.* This form of entertainment is called a moving picture because the people and things you see in it appear to move as they do in real life. A movie camera is used to film the pictures for a movie. The images are recorded on a very long strip of plastic film. A movie camera takes photographs in the same way as an ordinary still camera. But it takes them very quickly, one after another, and spaces them along the film. The actors' voices are recorded on **magnetic tape.** The pictures and sounds are recorded in small chunks called **takes.** There is a piece of film for each take.

Inside a modern theater. The screen is behind a fireproof curtain.

Movie sets look disorganized, but each person is doing a particular job.

The Editor

A film editor puts together the final film. The editor starts with all the pieces of film and the sound tapes. He or she selects the good bits of film, throws the bad bits away, and joins everything together. The sound and any special effects are also added to the film.

At the Theater

The film arrives at the theater in two or three long rolls called **reels**. A projector shines light through the film, which enables you to see the picture on the screen. The projector also plays the film's sound.

Try to imagine the months or years of work that have gone into making the next action movie you see.

ONE MAN, MANY INVENTIONS!

Thomas Alva Edison (1847–1931) was a famous American inventor. He invented the first sound recording machine and the microphone and built the first electric power station. He also invented the kinetoscope, which showed motion pictures. Only one person at a time could view the pictures through a small eyepiece.

MOVING PICTURES

Look at something in the room and then close your eyes tightly very quickly. You will find that your eyes "remember" what you were looking at for a split second before everything goes dark. This effect is called **persistence of vision**, and movies depend on it. A movie is made up of thousands of pictures, each one slightly different from the one before. Each picture is called a **frame**. When you watch the movie, you see the frames one after the other in quick succession. In fact, you see 24 frames every second. Persistence of vision means that you do not see the gaps between the frames, and you are fooled into thinking you are seeing a moving picture.

THOUSANDS OF FRAMES

A movie is filmed and shown at the rate of 24 frames every second. A movie that lasts for an hour and a half (90 minutes) contains 90 × 60 × 24 = 129,600 frames! The actual film is more than 1.8 miles long.

Early Toys

In the middle of the 19th century, before movies were ever thought of, toys that produced moving pictures were very popular with children (and adults!). The toys made use of persistence of vision, just as modern movies do. The simplest toy was called a thaumatrope. It was a disc with a picture on each side. When you spun the disc, the two pictures appeared quickly, one after the other, and combined into one picture. Other toys, such as the zoetrope and phenakistiscope, showed moving pictures made up of 10 or more frames. All the pictures were drawn by hand, because there were no movie cameras to film real objects as they moved.

This is a zoetrope. When you spin the cylinder and look through the slots, you see a moving picture.

First Photos

Photography started early in the 19th century. At that time, scientists realized that certain chemicals change into other chemicals when light shines on them. Early photographs were taken over a period of several minutes, because the chemicals changed only very slowly. Photographic chemicals were gradually improved, and by the 1870s photographs could be taken in less than a second. By this time, photographers could take pictures quickly, one right after another, and record moving things. In the 1890s a French scientist, Etienne Jules Marey, built a movie camera and projector. He used them to record and show the movement of animals and people in **slow motion**.

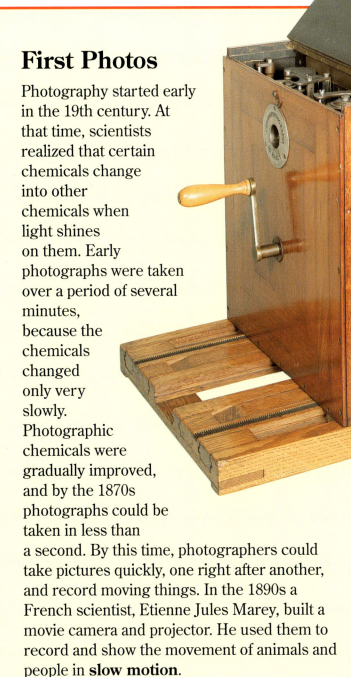

Marey's movie camera and projector of the 1890s was able to record and show slow-motion movement.

This piece of Marey's work shows a man jumping, in slow motion. You can see each move made in the jump.

7

ON FILM

Have you ever wondered how film records action? Moving pictures are photographed by movie cameras. The camera's job is to take a photograph, wind the film inside the camera, take another photograph, wind the film again, and so on. The **lens** at the front of the camera collects light from the scene being photographed and shines it onto the film. The film contains chemicals that change into different chemicals when light hits them. Where more light reaches the film, the chemicals change more. In this way, the film records the scene.

In Focus

We see an object because our eyes detect some of the light rays that are reflected from it. At the front of each eye there is a lens. It collects light rays from a scene and shines them onto the light-sensitive retina at the back of each eye. A movie camera works in the same way. Its lens bends the rays so that all the rays coming from one place in the scene hit the same place on the film. This makes a sharp, clear, focused image on the film. If the rays do not hit the same place on the film the image is blurred. The camera's shutter opens to let light hit the film, and then closes when the film is winding.

The large drums on a movie camera contain hundreds of feet of film.

Two rays from each point in the scene are focused onto the film.

Zoom In and Out

Most movie cameras have a zoom lens. It allows the filmmaker to get a close-up view of actors' faces, for example, or to show a wide view of a scene.

A zoom lens can work like a telescope so that just a small part of the scene appears, magnified, in the image. This is called telephoto. The lens can also make a very large area of the scene appear, reduced, in the image. This is called wide angle.

UNDERWATER CAMERAS

As a diver goes deeper under water, water presses harder on the diver's body. The same **pressure** acts on underwater cameras. They have strong metal cases with rubber seals to withstand the pressure, so water does not leak into the camera. They are painted yellow so they can be seen in the gloomy deep-sea light.

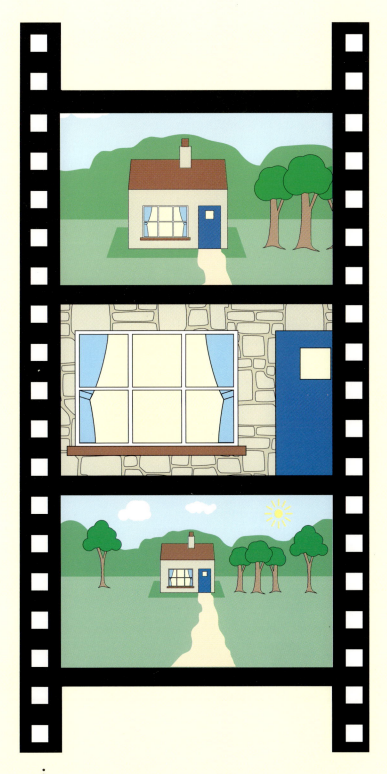

Top: the normal view of a scene
Middle: the view with the zoom set to telephoto
Bottom: the view with the zoom set to wide angle

SOUNDTRACKS

As you watch a movie, you hear the soundtrack at the same time. The soundtrack is normally contained on a narrow strip of magnetic material down the side of the film, next to the frames of pictures. It is like having the tape from an audiocassette glued along the film. The soundtrack is recorded onto the film by making magnetic patterns in the strip. When the film is shown, the sound is reproduced by loudspeakers in the theater. But how is the sound recorded in the first place?

A Sound Recording

When something makes a noise, it makes the air around it vibrate, or move. The vibrations spread out quickly. You can hear the sound when the vibrations reach your ears. On a film set, the actors' voices are picked up by microphones. These turn the sounds into **electric signals**, which are recorded on a magnetic tape. Sometimes voices are recorded after filming has been completed in a process called **dubbing**. The movie's music and sound effects are recorded on other tapes. All the sounds are then mixed together by a sound engineer to make the final soundtrack.

To collect sounds, the sound technician holds the microphone near the actors. It is supported on a long pole called a boom.

Sound on Film

A movie's soundtrack is sometimes recorded on the film as a pattern of light and dark. Inside the projector, a light is shone through the film. A light detector on the other side detects the changing light pattern and turns it into an electric signal. The signal is sent to the loudspeakers, which change it back into the sounds we hear.

IN TIME

The pictures and sounds on the final film must be exactly in time with each other. The process of making sure that this happens is called synchronization. A clapper board is snapped shut in front of the camera at the start of each take. The point on the picture frame where it closes can be matched with the soundtrack because of the snapping noise that it makes.

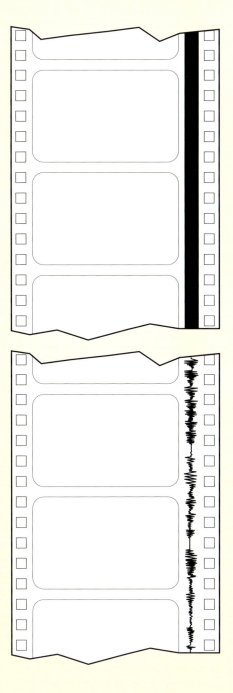

Top: a magnetic soundtrack on a film
Bottom: an optical soundtrack on a similar film.

BRIGHT LIGHTS

Movie sets and film studios always have plenty of bright lights. Why are these bright lights, called lamps, needed? It is mainly because lighting makes the scene bright enough for the film in the movie camera to record it. The lights do the same job as a flash on a normal camera. Lighting is especially important in a studio or on a dull day outdoors. Filmmakers also use lighting to create dramatic scenes. Spotlights can light up just one area of a scene, and colored lamps can make actors and sets look weird or spooky.

A Beam of Light

Every lamp has a bulb. Inside the bulb is a thin coil of wire called a filament. When electricity flows through the filament, the filament gets so hot that it glows very brightly. Light spreads out in all directions from the bulb. A mirror behind the bulb reflects any light going backward, and sends it out of the front of the lamp. Spotlights also have a lens at the front to direct the light into a narrow beam.

Low-angle spot lighting creates a tall, spooky shadow of the actress and the stair railing.

Here, lighting comes from the sun and spotlights. Extra light can be shone on the scene by large, flat white sheets called reflectors.

Colors and Filters

Sunlight is made from a mixture of many different colors of light. It is called white light. You can see the different colors of light in a rainbow. The light bulbs that you use at home give out light that is quite yellow. If this kind of bulb were used to light a movie set, the final picture would look too yellow. Movie lamps, like other photographic lamps, produce natural-looking white light. Colored light is made by sliding a **filter** over the lamp. The filter stops light rays of all the colors except for the color needed, which it lets pass through.

A spot of colored light produced by a spotlight and colored filter

LIGHT POWER

The power of a light is measured in the number of watts of electricity that it uses. A flashlight bulb has a power of about 1 watt (1 W). Light bulbs you use at home have a power of between 40 and 100 watts. A movie-set lamp has a power of several thousand watts.

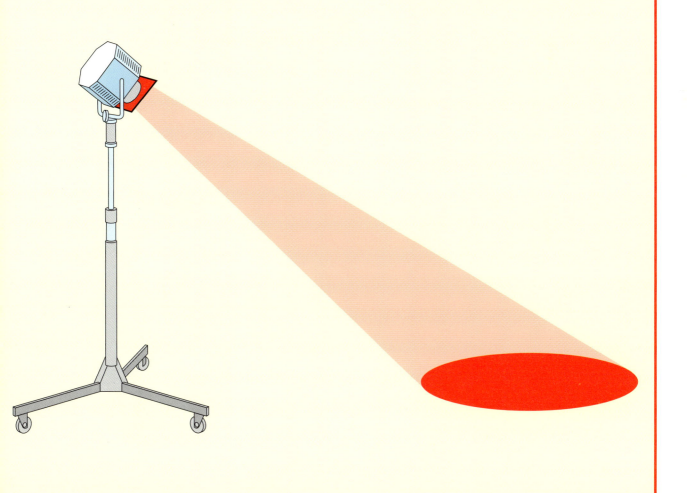

FROM CAMERA TO THEATER

What happens to a film after it has been used in a movie camera? The chemicals on the film contain the images of each frame of the moving picture. They are not images that you can see but simply patterns of different chemicals in the film. The film must be kept in complete darkness. If any light gets onto it, the chemicals will change again and the images will be ruined. The film is taken to a processing laboratory. Here it goes through a chemical process that turns the chemical images into real pictures that you can see.

A commercial movie film processing laboratory. The film moves gradually through tanks of chemicals.

Color Films

All the colors of the rainbow can be made up by mixing red, blue, and green light together, in different amounts. A color film has three layers: one is sensitive to blue light, one to red light, and one to green light. Yellow light, for example, is a mixture of red and green light. When the camera films a yellow object, the red and green layers of the film react, but the blue layer does not. When this film is developed, the red layer turns red and the green layer turns green where the light has hit the film. When light shines through the developed film, the colored layers act as filters and turn the light into the right color.

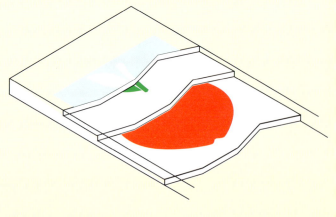

Here is a cut-away of a developed color film. The layers are supported by plastic.

A film editor at work. The editing machine allows quick and accurate cutting and splicing.

Film Editing

A movie is not filmed in one long take. Takes can be a few seconds or a few minutes long, and there may be several takes for the same scene. When the film is processed, a film editor selects the best pieces and joins them together to make the final film. This is done by cutting between the frames and joining, or splicing, them together with tape. Finally, the film is copied on to one or two long pieces of film. It is then copied again lots of times and sent out to be shown in theaters.

LOST FILMS

Early movies were photographed on film that gradually deteriorated, or lost its quality, as the chemicals on it reacted with the air. Many movies have been lost because the film has been destroyed this way. Movies today are photographed on film that does not deteriorate.

SPECIAL EFFECTS

How did the toys in *Toy Story* come to life? How did the dinosaurs in *Jurassic Park* run? The answer is by special effects. Special effects are produced by photographic tricks and computer graphics.

Flying on Film

Special effects experts have had several different ways of making actors in a studio look as though they are somewhere completely different. To show a person flying through the air, for example, the actor is filmed in a flying position in a studio. The background is shot on another piece of film. The two films are then mixed photographically to make the actor appear to be flying across the background. A "hole" is created in the background, which is then filled by the "flying" actor. Today, computers are used instead. First, the different pieces of film are scanned and stored in the computer. The scanning process divides the picture into millions of tiny colored squares. Any bits of film from one take can be cut out and added to another take. Finally, a special printer turns the computer images back into real film.

Special effects allow Superman and Lois Lane to fly above the earth.

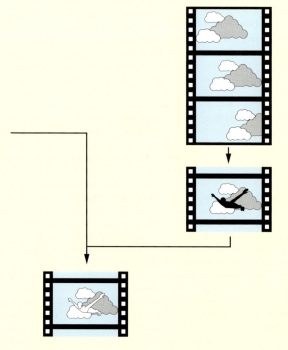

Actors are normally filmed against a plain background. This makes it easier to cut their images out of the background and add them on to another one.

Computer Effects

Computers can produce very convincing pictures of real or imaginary creatures and scenes. These can also be mixed with real **footage**. Filmmakers use computers to create amazing special effects. People can use computers to draw pictures of anything—and it doesn't have to be a drawing of a thing that exists in the real world. Once a model of, say, a dinosaur has been created inside the computer, the dinosaur can be viewed from any angle and with any sort of lighting. If the dinosaur created by computer is to be mixed with real film, the real lighting and the lighting of the computer image must be carefully matched.

AMAZING MOVIES

Stephen Spielberg (born 1946) is one of the most successful modern movie producers. His movies include *Jaws*, *E.T.*, and *Jurassic Park*. Most of his movies contain amazing special effects.

Roger Rabbit was created by computer and mixed into the real footage. Of course the actor, Bob Hoskins, had to imagine Roger was there.

STUNT ACTION

Although many special effects are created with camera tricks or computer, others are produced with models and slow-motion filming. Some dangerous pieces of action still have to be performed by specially trained people. They are known as stunt people. When they drive in car chases, jump from windows, or run through fires, stunt people need to work with great care and split-second timing.

Stunts

Stunt people have to understand how things fall, fly, burn, skid, and so on so that their stunts look real. At the same time the stunts need to be as safe as possible to perform. For a simple stunt, such as a fall from a roof, the stunt person lands on a soft mattress. The greater the drop, the faster the stunt person is traveling when he or she reaches the ground, and so the deeper the cushion needs to be. When stunts involve cars flying off cliffs or turning over on ramps, careful calculations are made to figure out where the car will land.

Fire Safety

Many action films involve fires and explosions. Sometimes stunt people have to go into a fire or be set on fire. They wear fire-resistant clothing that helps to protect them until the take is finished. The flames are put out with fire extinguishers immediately after the take. To create an explosion, the amount of explosive used is carefully calculated so that it produces a good effect without endangering the actors or film crew.

Filming a scene from the movie *Backdraft*. Stage hands are close by with fire extinguishers.

Models like this hand have to be made and filmed very carefully and as realistically as possible so that they look lifelike and scary.

Model Stunts

Filmmakers use models of things such as sinking ships or crashing aircraft for some action sequences. Special filming techniques are needed, however, to make them look real. Special-effects technicians understand that all objects fall downward at the same rate when they are dropped. For example, a real helicopter would fall in the same way as a much smaller model one. But if the model is filmed normally, it will appear to fall unnaturally fast, so it is photographed with the film running more quickly than normal. When the film is viewed at normal speed, the action looks natural.

A TRUE STORY?

In the movie *True Lies*, an actor jumps from a skyscraper onto the top of a Harrier jet hovering outside a building. In reality, the actor, aircraft, and skyscraper were all filmed separately. The three films were put together on a computer to create the scene you see in the movie.

ANIMATED MOVIES

How do filmmakers create cartoons? How do they bring puppets and models to life? The answer is by animation, the process of making inanimate (non-living) objects appear to move. Animated films are made by photographing cartoon pictures or models one by one. Each photograph makes up one frame of the film. After each frame, the cartoon pictures or models are moved a tiny bit, then another frame is photographed, and so on. This method of filming is called stop-frame photography. When the final film is viewed at the correct speed, you are tricked into thinking you are seeing a moving picture.

The popular British Wallace and Gromit films are created by stop-frame photography.

Cartoons on the Draw

To make a cartoon, a separate picture is drawn for each frame. Each frame is slightly different from the one before it. The characters and backgrounds are drawn separately on see-through plastic sheets called cells. This means that the background does not have to be drawn again and again. The background can be split into different parts and moved slightly along in each frame to make it look like movement.

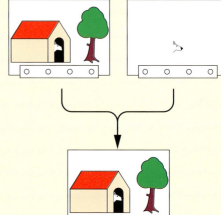

Shown here are animation cells. The kennel is drawn just once, but a bit moreof the dog can be seen in each frame.

Computer Cartoons

Today, many cartoons are drawn by computer. Artists sketch the shapes of the film's characters, which are then copied into the computer and colored. The artist draws a picture for every few frames, and the computer works out what the frames in between need to look like to make the characters' movements smooth. When the cartoon is complete, the frames are transferred from the computer onto film.

Models and Puppets

Models and puppets can be animated by photographing them in one position, moving them slightly and photographing them again. Animators must understand how people and animals move in real life in order to make them look real to us when we see the film. Model animation is filmed by fixing a camera to a **dolly** or tripod in a studio. The camera can be moved and zoomed for each step.

DISNEY FILMS

Walt Disney (1901–1966) was the most famous pioneer of animated films. In 1928 he created the cartoon character Mickey Mouse, and his film *Snow White and the Seven Dwarfs*, made in 1938, was the first full-length animated movie.

The pink figure is being animated. The camera is specially prepared to take stop-frame photographs.

ON SCREEN

Have you ever wondered how movies are shown at the theater? At the back of the theater is a projector. It shines light through the film and onto the theater screen, making a huge copy of the image that is on the film. Light hits the screen and bounces off into your eyes so you can see the image. The projector shows each frame of the film for just a fraction of a second before moving the film onto the next frame for a fraction of a second, and so on.

The Projector

The projector has a very powerful lightbulb that makes an extremely bright white light. This light is needed to produce a picture on the screen that is bright enough for you to see. A lens collects the light rays from the bulb and shines them onto the back of the film. When the light passes through the film, it becomes colored. The projector lens focuses the light rays onto the screen. It makes sure that light rays from the same point on the film strike the same point on the screen.

Inside the projection room of a theater. The pictures are projected through the window in the front wall.

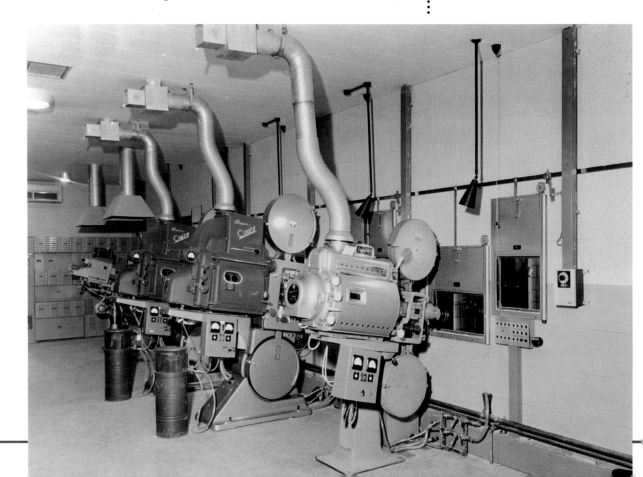

The Screen

The theater screen reflects light rays from the projector back into the eyes of the audience. It scatters the rays so that you see them coming from all parts of the screen, wherever you are sitting in the theater. Close up, the screen is quite rough, like a sheet of sandpaper. If the screen was very smooth, light rays hitting one part of the screen would bounce off toward some people in the audience and not others.

Sound

The film's soundtrack is picked up by the projector, which turns it into an electric signal. The signal is sent to loudspeakers. The speakers turn the electric signal into vibrating sound waves that you can hear. The speakers are normally placed behind the screen, which has thousands of tiny holes in its surface. The sound vibrations travel through these holes. In larger theaters, the **acoustics** of the building are designed so that no **echoes** are reflected from large flat areas such as the walls or ceiling. The ceiling is often covered in objects specially shaped to scatter the sound.

KEEPING COOL

Bright lights make a lot of heat. The heat from a projector lamp can make the film buckle (crumple), because the darker parts of the film become hot and expand. Cool air is blown across the film to prevent this from happening.

Shown here is a projector creating an image on a theater screen. The lens can move backward and forward to produce a clear image.

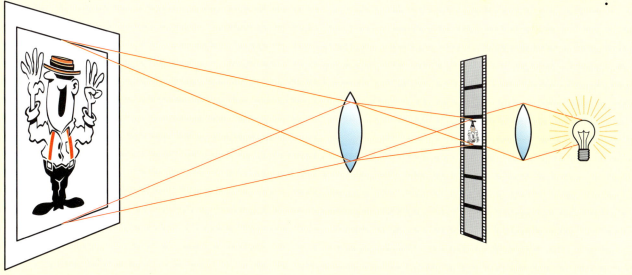

BIG PICTURES

Movie pictures are not all the same size and shape. The pictures that you watch on the theater screen are rectangular and usually measure about 30 feet wide and about 23 feet high. In the 1950s and 1960s, wide-screen movies were popular. Wide screens give the audience a much better feeling of being on the actual movie set. Recently, movie makers have used screens that are so big that they fill your whole **field of vision**. This means that you cannot see the sides of the screen, and your brain is fooled into thinking that you are really in the scene. Some screens are almost 100 feet high and wide and cover one whole wall of the theater.

Film Formats

The width of a roll of film, and the way in which the frames and soundtrack fit onto it, are called the film **format**. Most movies are photographed on 35-millimeter (mm) film (which is 35 mm wide). Wide-screen and IMAX formats are photographed on film that is 70 mm wide.

Wide-screen Movies

Cinerama and CinemaScope were two kinds of wide-screen movies invented in the 1950s and popular during the 1960s. Cinerama worked by projecting three films next to each other on a huge curved screen. Three cameras were used to film each scene of the movie. A CinemaScope camera had a special lens that squashed a wide scene into a normal-sized frame. The projector's lens reversed the process. Wide-screen movies became less popular in the 1970s.

The Cinerama wide-screen system was perfect for showing the natural world and action rides.

IMAX Movies

Large-screen movies are photographed on large-format film to produce an enormous and very clear picture. They are known as IMAX (Image Maximum) movies. If a normal film is shown at this size, it looks dim and blurred, because not enough detail has been recorded on the film itself. Because the picture on the large screen is so huge, a tiny vibration in the projector can make the picture shake. To avoid this, IMAX projectors are very heavy. They are mounted on rubber feet to help stop the vibrations.

Inside an IMAX theater, the screen is as tall as seven elephants standing on top of each other!

THEATER IN THE ROUND

In 1955 Walt Disney built a circular theater that gave an all-around, 360-degree view. It took 11 projectors to show the pictures. The audience stood in the middle of the circle.

MORE MOVIE TRICKS

Showing films on huge screens is one way of making a movie seem more like real action. What other tricks do movie makers use to make movies seem real?

Three-Dimensional Movies

The images in a three-dimensional (3-D) movie look like real, solid objects rather than just flat pictures. As your eyes are set a few inches apart, each eye sees a slightly different view of a scene. This allows you to see things in three **dimensions** and to judge how far away objects are. Photographs and movies look flat, because each eye sees the same picture. 3-D movies are photographed by two cameras side by side. One photographs the view your right eye would see, while the other photographs the view your left eye would see. In the theater, two projectors project the film onto the same screen. The projectors are fitted with special colored filters, and the audience wears glasses with filters of the same color. One eye sees light from one projector, and the other eye sees light from the other projector. Your brain is fooled into seeing the scenes in three dimensions.

This audience is watching a 3-D movie through special glasses.

The screens these theme-park riders are watching are inside their helmets. This is called virtual reality. Motion-control seats make it more realistic.

Simulator Rides

Many theme parks have simulator rides. On the ride, you sit in a seat and watch a movie that completely fills your field of vision. As you watch the movie you feel as if you are hurtling through a landscape, that you are part of the action. To add to the effect, your seat moves under you at the same time. This fools your senses of touch and balance as well as your sight. The effect can be frighteningly realistic! Some theaters have been built with motion-control seats.

HOW MANY FRAMES?

A team of American movie makers has carried out experiments to see how viewers' brains react to movies filmed at different **frame rates**. They found that a rate of 60 frames a second (instead of the normal 24) gives the most realistic effect.

MOVIES ABOUT SCIENCE

You have already seen how science plays a part in making and showing movies. But how do scientific things themselves appear in the movies? Movie makers try to make the science in their films as convincing as possible. They ask scientists from many different subject areas—physicists, biologists, medical experts, and so on—to advise them when they are writing scripts and building movie sets and **props**.

Fact or Fiction?

Unfortunately, knowledge about science facts sometimes makes it difficult to make a good, exciting movie! Sometimes they have to be ignored as, for example, in movies about such fantastic subjects as the monster created by Dr. Frankenstein; the monster is built from parts of dead people and brought to life with electricity! Or the audience has to believe that the characters in the movie have developed new scientific techniques or new technologies. Real scientists do not believe that dinosaurs can be brought back to life as they were in *Jurassic Park*. And in the movies, computers always seem to be much more clever than they are in real life!

New scientific techniques made dinosaurs come back to life in *Jurassic Park*.

Journey to the Moon was made in 1902, 67 years before the first moonwalk. In it, a professor is launched to the moon in a large bullet fired from a cannon.

Fiction to Fact

Science-fiction movies are about aliens, future worlds, and time travel. Movie makers invent scientific ideas and technologies to include in their films. They make their fictional ideas convincing to us by basing them on actual scientific ideas. Some of the earliest films were science-fiction movies. The ideas in them, such as people flying to the moon, must have seemed ridiculous when the movies were first made. Yet many have already come true. Perhaps we shall bring a tyrannosaurus back to life one day!

SPACE GARBAGE

In the 1995 film *Apollo 13*, the damaged Apollo spacecraft drifts through space, leaving behind a trail of debris from an explosion on board. In reality, this could never happen – the debris would drift along with the spacecraft!

GLOSSARY

acoustics the study of sound. The acoustics of a room describe the way in which sound travels around it.

dimension the size of an object in one direction or another. A movie screen has two dimensions—length and width. A three-dimensional movie has depth from front to back as well.

dolly a platform on wheels for a television or movie camera

dubbing the process of adding voices to a movie after the original pictures have been shot without recording the voices. The actors watch themselves on the film and speak the lines to match.

echo a reflected sound. Echoes happen when sound vibrations reach a solid surface and bounce back off it.

electric signal an electric current that changes its strength and direction. In sound-recording equipment, the changes represent the vibrations of the sound.

field of vision the whole area of a scene that you can see at one time without moving your eyes up or down or from side to side

filter a piece of glass or plastic that changes any light shining through it. Color filters stop some colors of light and let other colors pass through.

footage a piece of film. The word *footage* comes from *foot*, which is used to measure the length of a piece of film.

format the size of a film and the way in which the frames and soundtrack are organized on it

frame a single photograph in a sequence on a film

frame rate the number of frames of a film that are shown in each second. Most films are shown at a rate of 24 frames a second.

lens a piece of glass or clear plastic that bends light rays as they pass through it. All optical instruments, such as cameras, telescopes, and microscopes, use lenses.

magnetic tape a ribbon of thin plastic. It is coated with material that can be magnetized. Sound and other information can be recorded on the tape by making a magnetic pattern.

persistence of vision the way that your eyes "remember" a scene for a split second, even when they can no longer see the scene. Movies appear to move because of persistence of vision.

pressure the amount of force (a force is a push or a pull) that presses on a certain area. As you go down in water, the water pressure pushing down on you increases because of the weight of the water above you.

props objects, such as furniture and vehicles, that are put in a film set to make it look like a real-life scene

reel a long piece of film that is rolled up tightly. Films are stored in reels inside lightproof containers.

set an area where actors perform in front of cameras. A set can be a real one, either indoors or outdoors, or built in a studio.

slow motion the slowed-down movement on a film. The effect is made by filming the action at a certain frame rate and then projecting it at a slower frame rate.

take a short piece of action that is filmed. Filmmakers film several takes of the same scene and then choose the best take during editing.

FACT FILE

- The first successful talking movie, or "talkie" was *The Jazz Singer*, made in 1927. Before then, lines of speech appeared on the screen for the viewers to read, and a musician in the theater played live music.

- Korea has the largest theater screen in the world. It is 108 feet wide and 92 feet high.

- The first public film show was presented in Paris, France, in 1895, by Louis and Auguste Lumière. The short films were about everyday life in Paris.

- Movies were originally thought of as just an interesting amusement. Louis Lumière said: "Cinema is a technology without a future."

- The longest movie ever made lasted 48 hours. It was called *The Longest Most Meaningless Movie in the World*.

- The Radio City Music Hall, in New York, is the world's largest theater. It has 5,874 seats.

FURTHER READINGS

Acona, George. *My Camera.* Crown Publisher, Inc., 1992.

Lambert, Mark. *TV and Video Technology.* Bookwright Press, 1990.

Scott, Elaine. *Movie Magic: Behind the Scenes with Special Effects.* Morrow, 1995.

INDEX

acoustics 23
animation 20–21
Apollo 13 29

Backdraft 18
background 16
boom 10

cartoons 20–21
cells 20
CinemaScope 24
Cinerama 24
clapper board 11
color film 14
colors 13, 14
computer graphics 16, 17, 19, 20, 21
cutting 15

Disney, Walt 21, 25
dolly 21
dubbing 10

echo 23
Edison, Thomas Alva 5
electric signal 10, 11, 23
E.T. 17

field of vision 24, 27
filament 12
film developing 14
film editing 5, 15
film formats 24
film studios 12
filter 13, 14, 26

fire extinguishers 18
fire-resistant clothing 18
fire safety 18
focus 8, 22
footage 17
frame 6, 11, 14, 20, 22, 27
frame rates 6, 27

IMAX 24, 25

Jaws 17
Jazz Singer, The 31
Journey to the Moon 29
Jurassic Park 16, 17, 28

kinetoscope 5

lamps 12
lens 8, 9, 12, 22, 24
light 22, 23
lighting 12–13
light power 13
Longest Most Meaningless Movie in the World, The 31
loudspeakers 10, 11, 23

magnetic tape 4, 10
Marey, Etienne Jules 7
Mickey Mouse 21

microphone 10
motion-control seat 27
movie camera 4

persistence of vision 6
phenakistiscope 6
photographic chemicals 7, 8, 14, 15
photographic tricks 16, 26
photography 7
pressure 9
processing laboratory 14
projector 5, 11, 22, 24, 25, 26
props 28
puppets 21

reels 5

science-fiction film 29
screen 5, 22, 23, 24
set 4, 10, 12, 24, 28
shutter 8
slow motion 7, 18
Snow White and the Seven Dwarfs 21
sound 10-11
sound engineer 10
soundtrack 10-11, 23
special effects 15-16, 19

Spielberg, Stephen 17
splicing 15
spotlight 12
stop-frame photography 20
stunts 18-19, 21
synchronization 11

take 4, 11, 15, 16, 18
telephoto lens 9
thaumatrope 6
theater 10, 22, 23, 31
three-dimensional (3-D) movies 26
Toy Story 16
True Lies 19

underwater cameras 9

watts 13
white light 13, 22
wide screen 24
wide-angle lens 9

zoetrope 6
zoom lens 9